Tokonoma

Also by José Kozer at Shearsman Books

Anima

Tokonoma (bilingual edition)

José Kozer

Tokonoma

translated by Peter Boyle

Shearsman Books

First published in the United Kingdom in 2014 by
Shearsman Books
50 Westons Hill Drive
Emersons Green
BRISTOL
BS16 7DF

Shearsman Books Ltd Registered Office
30–31 St. James Place, Mangotsfield, Bristol BS16 9JB
(this address not for correspondence)

www.shearsman.com

ISBN 978-1-84861-385-0
Original text copyright © José Kozer, 2011.
Translation copyright © Peter Boyle, 2014.

The right of José Kozer to be identified as the author, and of Peter Boyle
to be identified as the translator, of this work has been asserted by them
in accordance with the Copyrights, Designs and Patents Act of 1988.
All rights reserved.

ACKNOWLEDGEMENTS
Tokonoma was first published by
Amargord Ediciones, Madrid, 2011.

This edition appears simultaneously with a fully bilingual version
under ISBN 978-1-84861-374-4,

Contents

Wo	9

I

The Concentration of Chang Hsu	13
Concentration of Chu Hsi	17
The Concentration of Tu Fu	19
Concentration of Wang Wei	22
Concentration of Master Kuan Hsiu	25
Concentration of Master Ning	28
Concentration of Go Toba	31
Concentration ('In the sky Sagittarius')	36
Concentration ('He leans')	37

II

Meditation ('The monk Noin')	41
Meditation ('Cowbell')	43
Meditation ('For a year now')	44
Meditation ('The/ attention')	48
Meditation ('With the utmost care')	49
Meditation of Kiyowara Fukayabu	51

III

Contemplation ('During the worst snowfall')	57
Contemplation ('The window. From the bed')	59

IV

Satori ('Hsin, of the Shingon sect')	65
Satori ('Hui-neng, tegument')	66
Satori ('Hui-neng, sixth patriarch')	70
Satori ('Noin contemplates')	72
Satori ('The rollcall of the Masters')	75
Satori ('The arhat knows')	79
Satori ('Ducks/ come')	82
Satori ('The entrance to the Temple')	85
Satori ('Po Chu-I has set down')	88

Satori ('Elegance of Fujiwara no Teika')	91
Satori (Ryokan)	93
Satori ('From/ the peg')	96
Satori ('The marigolds that adorned')	100
Satori (Ma Non Troppo)	103
Satori ('He imagined')	108
Satori ('He walked thinking')	110
Satori ('He adjusts his step')	113
Satori (Overnight/ my pubic hair)	117
Satori ('Under the hundred year old…')	118
Satori ('The/ monk')	120

V.

Satori ('The/ worm')	125
Satori ('I'm/ going/ to be born')	126
Portrait of a seventy year old and an adolescent	130

Wo

The philosopher Mo Tse teaches: refuting me is like
    firing eggs at a rock.

You can use up all the eggs but the rock remains unharmed.

The philosopher Wo uses up all the eggs of the world
    against a rock
    and conquers it.

First, to make the rock memorable.

Second, because in the future, given its
    excess yellowness,
    whoever approaches
    the rock confuses the
    moon and horses.

And third, even more importantly: one verdict
    acts on another
    verdict,

cancels the obsession of its words.

I

The Concentration of Chang Hsu

Taking off your shirt demands measure.

The act of defecation involves the respiratory
        system, concerns
        every detail of
        the organism.

Positioning yourself in a chair in the early hours
        of morning must be
        considered a transcendental
        moment, all too easily
        disturbed: it requires
        character (agility)
        all at once your
        concentration
        shifts from knees
        to groin, adjusting
        the body's posture
        from waist upward.

Chang Hsu transmits to us other rules (more
        far more than a thousand
        have been counted): his
        words, registered
        for posterity (Chang
        Hsu surrounded by
        the Immortals of Wine
        laughed and called
        posterity posteriority) his
        words divide matter, and
        the skein of matter, into
        what makes sense and
        what does not: Chang

> identifies good sense
> with working in the fields,
> the life of birds, the insects'
> (comfortable, relaxed) way
> of busying themselves:
> modest creatures.
> The absence of good sense
> remains, obviously, for
> those with two hands.

To correct the lack of good sense corresponds to the rules:
> these can be reduced to two
> or three laws that are one;
> or you can study them
> and put them into practice
> over a long life, one
> by one, day by
> day, from the precise
> proliferation of the thousand
> and one rules aimed
> at, smoothly, firmly,
> sustaining and continuing
> to sustain the guiding
> thread of attention, a
> tributary source
> of happiness.

Chang Hsu is not a model of anything, emulated no one,
> never considered he should
> be emulated. He got rid of
> the calligrapher's shirt,
> revised his thought,
> imperturbably took part
> in the morning's ablutions,
> and sat on a hemp
> mat, alone with
> the Immortals of Wine:

    house wine, fermented
    (from rice) five
    years in pewter
    barrels: one day he'd
    drink distilled wine,
    the next clouded.

A lightning flash, he opens his eyes: the same rooster at
    the same hour, some rats
    stirring restless in the
    straw.

Chang Hsu lets go, is empty. First ideogram (head shaven)
    a blackish coloured tunic.
    Second ideogram (his
    head inclined) one
    eye only. Second cup
    of wine, Chang Hsu
    now lighter (laughing,
    all by himself, blurted
    out to the members of
    the Community of
    Wine last night that
    he didn't drink myths,
    only wine and water)
    (water, he pointed out, that
    other form of calm). Third
    ideogram, the ideogram then
    of water. Were these hours,
    these days, flowcharts?
    Leaning on the window sill
    Chang looks at the flowerbed
    of invasive chickweed,
    notices its flowering,
    considers he will have to
    come closer to inspect
    them thoroughly when

the sun goes down: the
most insignificant wildflower
requires a specific inflorescence, the
chickweed require the cusp
of an ideogram, two cups
(more) of rice wine,
to lighten tomorrow's
body.

Concentration of Chu Hsi

Master Chu Hsi recommends taking seven
        words at random (from
        the dictionary?) (well,
        ok, yes, from the
        dictionary) to know
        the future.

(We are born? Yeah, sure. We die? Yeah, sure.
        And next what? What
        do you mean,
        next what?)

(Master Chu Hsi arms crossed, a fire, a few
        half cold embers, two
        sweet potatoes, burning
        dung, *chu* (candle)
        cheers: the cup of wine
        suddenly strikes
        the mat (six palms wide)
        (made from woven
        rattan).

(Acerola (not casserole, acerole) hayloft carpenter's plane
        carabao sandalwood
        scarcely clog).

(Ah, Chance. Disciple Chu Shu-chen has studied
        his future for twenty five
        years, where it says
        carpenter's plane
        a few shavings gather,
        carabao day by day
        inspires him
        to work.)

(Sandalwood smoke drives him mad for a month,
        lunar or solar he
        couldn't say. The pair
        of clogs, still dirty from
        blackened earth, at the
        foot of the deathbed,
        belonged to Master
        Chu Hsi).

(Chu Shu-chen imagines he can know his Future in
        advance, or at least
        go beyond the hidden
        meaning of the word
        clog in less than three
        lustra. And then?
        Ah no, what do you mean
        and then?).

Scarcely transmitting to his seven disciples the idea
        that a word like the
        word scarcely can
        scarcely transmit the
        notion of Future: at
        sixty he recommends
        sitting in the open
        air holding present
        in mind the word
        scarcely as if it
        were a cliff that not
        being eternal must
        in its own due time
        crumble (ah in its
        own due time,
        exclaim the seven
        disciples in unison).

The Concentration of Tu Fu

Tu Mu told Tu Fu he was disoriented.

Here in the mountains there are no roads, we
        rely solely on a tree
        that likes mountains,
        clearings and forests
        (thickets) the species
        reproduces and modifies
        so that the only
        existing bird, in all
        its mutations (which
        are only the air's
        business) should
        have a place to land,
        according to a law
        that has never been
        obeyed (the golden oriole
        was made to nest in
        willows, just as the wagtail
        should only sing lost in
        the thick tangle of the
        walnut tree).

Tu Mu doesn't stop scratching his head while
        Tu Fu continues his
        ruminations.

Huashan, a sacred peak, with much effort the peak
        is accessible, what's
        inaccessible usually is
        the sacred. Tu Fu
        explains to Tu Mu
        (who doesn't stop
        scratching his head)
        that exertion leads

              to disorientation.
              Disorientation
              means reasoning,
              means being at the
              temple's entrance
              and seeing cowsheds. Oh
              cowsheds and corner
              stores, weavers and
              grocers, spinning wheels
              and abacuses; proliferating
              flutes and bamboo
              cages with the bird
              that will bring joy to
              our mornings (like this,
              Tu Mu, no one will wake
              to the truth) unless
              we understand the
              meaning of the caged
              bird's song, the bird
              foretelling the unstoppable
              chain of events, listen
              to it from dawn to
              dusk and cover its
              cage with a black
              taffeta hood.

Tu Mu understands (Oh, not for the first time) Unity
              encompasses the totality
              of numbers (for a moment
              he stops scratching his
              head) and names lock
              us in a cage: that as Tu
              Fu has aptly explained
              isn't a matter of maples
              or almond trees in flower
              or finches and calandra
              larks but of the Tree

and the Bird where,
clearly, Tree is Bird, all
in the same bosom, an
undifferentiated abyss.

Tu Mu trembles all over when Tu Fu lands a slap
three times on his
cheeks (Tu Mu will
have raised his hands
to cover his head).

Tu Fu, after taking a few steps back, returns: places before
Tu Mu's anxious nostrils
three red hot objects,
pristine objects: the
leaf of a weeping willow;
a feather fallen from a
heron as perhaps
terrified it flew away:
and the ideogram
shih. Tu Fu indicates to
Tu Mu that he should
concentrate all his
attention first on the
left side of the ideogram,
later there'll be time to
speak of marriage,
ornate boxes with bridal
coins, the civil service
and its ranks, mushrooms
and woods, there will
be time to sit down at
the entrance to the
temple situated
(evidently) on the
right side (*shih*) of
the ideogram.

21

Concentration of Wang Wei

Wang Wei

paints as he writes, writes as he paints
        to avoid confusion,

alternatives.

He paints crane, immediately the crossword puzzle scrambles
        its five letters; he writes
        crane and the sheet of
        rice paper that should enter
        such mystical absorption,
        regains its whiteness:
        the bird (its trace
        still fresh) has flown.

Wang Wei

thinks the world, more than mysterious, is
        (as they like to say
        in the Peking dialect)
        a load of crap.

(Parenthesis: the words 'load of crap' scarcely transmit
        the original ideogram that
        makes Wang Wei smile so
        much: it approximates far
        more our national term,
        shit eater).

A sign

of the terse equanimity achieved by Wang Wei
        is that he doesn't stop

    painting as he writes,
    writing as he paints:
    you've got to wonder
    what heights of thought
    he has attained,
    it wouldn't

be fair

to reply for Wang Wei. And so, we step close
    (without cornering or
    bugging him) to check
    he's heard the question,
    recognises the intrinsic
    value of that category of
    question that tinges (stains)
    every type of answer.
    Wang

Wei

replies: you paint the crane and then it's not there,
    you write crane, then
    we confirm the word's
    not there either, and
    that at best the above-
    mentioned word
    signifies a gaggle of
    birds, item, compost
    for the fields. Must we
    despair? Wang

Wei

suggests (like it or not, you've got to live) that whoever paints
    as they write and writes
    as they paint, or whoever

        writes as they write and
        paints as they paint, has
        for an occupation not
        being a mender of old pans
        or rag-and-bone man (to
        bring in a few examples by
        way of comparison) relies

in the long run on the inexhaustible presence
        (recurrence) of blank
        rice paper, the
        whiteness of infinite

gaps.

Concentration of Master Kuan Hsiu

A waterwheel, sand falls.

A bucket, gravel flows.

Reversing the waterclock, the hourglass.

He opens his eyes slightly, a stream; he closes them,
        sandhills.

He trains fossilized birds, sterile plants.

He pulls out a few marsh marigolds by the roots, the
        (absent) beach crab
        has returned to
        its cave.

And if he amputates his arm, loam; and if he tears
        out his eye,
        clay.

Nonetheless he is made of comfortably seated, his voice
        faintly echoing, flesh,
        flesh that rises.

Master Kuan Hsiu stands up, poet, painter,
        calligrapher, embraced
        by the powerful,
        disciple of Buddha, a
        prodigious memory,
        precise biography, details
        written down, six seven
        servings of food a day
        varied with restraint,
        his balance has become
        emblematic for the

Kingdom, no wonder
the Emperor consults
him, eunuchs sand-
fearing bow as he
arrives, Master Kuan
Hsiu expounds, voice
of sand dunes, voice of
the wasteland, where he
interprets then exhorts,
in the gardens (lotus)
(miosotis) (beds of
marigolds) reveals the
stone, doesn't even
have to point with his
index finger, preaches
(relying on the Diamond
Sutra) on the destiny
of stone, destiny of
the bird dozing in
the date palms of an
oasis, an oasis
of sand destiny of
the palms, the
Emperor himself
will eat dates of sand,
applause, acclaim quartz
petals, only sand will
persevere, look, one
more hole, engrave,
engrave death on
one side, extinction
on the other, in
a hand-held chair
they convey him back
to his house, his
hermit's shack,
Master, if one might offer

you something, Master,
anything you need?, Kuan
Hsiu spins
around, starts
softly humming
seated on a palm
mat, he means a
sand mat, he meant
softly humming the
word sand, his mouth
filled with water.

Concentration of Master Ning

In order to vanish, in the morning Master Ning was
        a spider dedicated
        to weaving, at
        evening flowering
        sage bud number
        twenty two of a sprig
        that was starting to
        bend to the earth
        through an excess of
        flowering, and at night
        he was a fly in the eye
        of the web, a cow pat
        used as fertiliser for
        a row of sage in a
        flowerbed: finally he
        turned out to be a
        microorganism of
        regular shape, universal
        nature, bearing the
        thousand faces of
        the Buddha, he will
        be Buddha in the
        moment he becomes
        (unto himself)
        unnoticed.

Nothing easier, says Ning waking up. He is sitting
        at the foot of a stone
        bench behind the house,
        with his hand he cleans
        the surface of the stone
        (rounding it off) now
        there's no asking if the
        stone or the palm of his

hand (Ning was left-
handed) will wear away
first. He scrubs the stone,
kneads his hands, goes
back to his task: when
the spider will have
finished its everlasting
web, hand and stone
will have vanished.
Ning toils and is
immersed. He doesn't
concentrate since
he's reached the
concentration level of
non-existence. He doesn't
pretend to know the time
elapsed since the spider
made its final stitches,
his left hand has become
that clearness that
entices gods to take a
rest, the stone purefied
by friction was the
meagre emptiness
occupied by the sage
bed.

The last delights of Master Ning: the fall of sage flower number
twenty two, this joy
of intermediate
intensity consists
in contemplating
(self-contemplating)
the instant of breaking
off (in an arc) to touch
the ground (to become
one with it): joy of

the trajectory (lasting
a *kalpa*). After the *kalpa*
Ning sees the nun he
adores walk past heading
towards the eye of
the spider web (he always
knew the fly was
playing dead) joy of
Ning's last (eight
minute) penetration
of the nun. Broken stone.
Scarcely fertile sand.
Hand gone back to
stardust (so to speak):
gods non-existent
through excess godlike-ness
(truly the gods have
stopped having fun):
soon Ning will be the
microorganism that
precedes Nothingness.
The joy at last of a
penultimate step, he
is once more a
mosquito, he buzzes
round himself, the
mosquito threatens to
pierce his middle ear,
Ning (startled)
smashes it.

Concentration of Go Toba

Go Toba the Perfect, watch him, watch him, he lives
        concentrated.

He finishes settling his body's posture, adjusting
        to its unreality *obi*
        kimono tabi, his
        gaze on the vase he
        placed at the precise
        centre of the table,
        precise centre a
        great teaching.

Black vase with a white emblem at its precise centre,
        the width of the vase
        takes into account the
        the precise contents of
        the bunches of flowers,
        the ornamental fern,
        water to a fixed height
        predetermined by
        the ancestral rite of
        flower arrangement,
        art of moderation.

Go Toba has not moved one iota, out there the cuckoo
        perched on the branch
        nearest the lounge room
        window didn't move,
        no wind stirs, in the
        garden of pebbles not
        a single bud breaks
        open: the watchman
        sleeps wrapped in
        his blue tunic, the

>   monk with the rake
>   obviously rakes, will
>   it be worth the
>   trouble of substituting
>   the wide vase for a
>   narrow one where
>   a long-stemmed
>   (unchanging)
>   yellow rose fits
>   perfectly the dark
>   green frond of a
>   fern, a delicate branch
>   of ornamental red
>   maple?

The maple in the garden.

So finally, which vase this morning? Has the ablution
>   been done already, the
>   miso soup, the tea,
>   the rice cracker? In
>   what order? Does he
>   combine them alternately
>   or better first finish
>   the bowl of miso,
>   then eat the cracker,
>   and then, only then,
>   drink the cup of
>   strong breakfast tea,
>   the first of the day,
>   come on then, wake
>   up and appear
>   alert, fully ready for
>   concentration?

A shadow slides in. Go Toba blinks (Buddha did not
>   blink, a sign of
>   true concentration).

A narrow
vase
of white
porcelain
or
a red
translucent
vase
of
antique
glass,
a
red
or
yellow
rose,
a pink
rose,
half
closed
or
already
open
to
its
depths,
a

    small branch of sweet williams combined with a long
        vine covered in
        honeysuckle that
        must have been
        interwoven with
        supreme care
        between the leaves,
        buds, opening
        blossoms of the

        flower arrangement
        presented by
        the hand of

Go
Toba,
of
his
chief
steward,
and
by
the
hand
of
his
dead
mother,
dead
and
purely
a
speculation?

The cuckoo flew away, screaming with exasperation. Wind rose,
        the so-called North Wind:
        in the distance the drum
        major thundered,
        signalling what exactly?
        Go Toba suddenly
        recalls the losses
        incurred this year by
        the finance house that
        invests his capital,
        some time we're having.
        And some wealth of
        fauna circumscribing

Go Toba's concentration.
Everything throws him
off balance. Everything
is turned upside down,
all in a mess, out, out,
eyes bulging, kimono
come undone, *obi* on
the floor, Go Toba hurls
an ancestral curse at
the heavens, and with
his reading pointer
shatters table, living
room, vase, kicks
the flower (the kick
was the best of

all).

Concentration

In the sky Sagittarius bends his bow.

The sparrowhawk in the sky gets ready.

The wind whips the willow tree's irrepressible
        string.

Irrepressibly (above) the sun creeps.

It releases the bee; the bee's sting shakes up
        the pollen, the seed
        opens.

And it falls, it leaps: its straight line (yellow) curves in the
        sky it climbs on the
        strings of the willow,
        a straight line its
        diagonal crosses
        space (sparrowhawk,
        reversed) leaning
        over (celestial music)
        Sagittarius, reflects.

All facts and their impressions ricochet off
        its stone body.

Concentration

He leans his right hand on the book he's reading
       at the table.

His left hand, hanging free, now and
       then from one side
       then the other shoos
       off the constellations.

II

Meditation

The monk Noin evaluates squared, maybe
>   cubed, to the nth
>   power, his image
>   in the portrait next to
>   the fruit arrangement
>   that must be placed
>   at evening on the
>   *tokonoma*, maybe
>   on the altar with the
>   bronze figurine and
>   three small bells,
>   his notebook of
>   observations, the
>   book of meditations.

In a final dream of nature (in any case not a
>   theological dream) he
>   receives the blessing of
>   his mother after receiving
>   the Master's blessing
>   (bronze statue): he
>   contemplates the portrait,
>   its shining surface, its
>   instantaneous shimmering
>   (opacity) until its
>   removal.

Dissolution. Has the vanity of the flesh in
>   living flesh or vainly
>   in vain representation
>   been dissolved? Spots
>   before the eyes. Embers
>   among the burnt
>   remnants of paper,

>
> signs of mechanical
> devotion. He knows this.
> It doesn't affect him. Also
> it's a road to follow: a
> question of persistence.
> And he touches one of
> the three hand bells
> bringing its silvery
> tinkling close to his ear
> as far as the exact
> location of sleepiness.

He has fallen asleep, flesh and representation: matter
> reigns supreme, flaunting
> its moments: substance
> does not exist: the
> Prime Mover has
> no foundation, no
> function. Barely
> flesh. The portrait
> of Noin (who put it
> on the *tokonoma*?)
> keeps its power of
> astonishing while
> the monks bawl out
> their singing, and Noin
> washes his hands of
> it (lying stretched
> out) on the bonfire.

Meditation

Cowbell.

Ten strikes of the small bell against the gong,
        ten

strikes. Female raven

flutters above male, squirrel a few very rapid twists and turns
        chasing

squirrel: a noisy racket

the sparrows. Freezing weather loads the old sycamore's
        high branches
        with

icicles: dawn,

a high branch cracks, turned to stone. A silent

arrow, it

falls and the male raven flutters above the female,
        the squirrel's

momentary

retreat: the gong, ten voices. The samurai takes
        a step forward,

        trips over the
        Emperor's

shadow.

Meditation

For a year now he has sought out night.

He sprawls comfortably in the grey canvas chair with
        its reinforced back
        (white pine) the city
        lights, the height of
        the terrace, searches
        the darkness, running
        his eye along the
        invisible pathway of
        the stars, recites a few
        lines by Yoka Daishi
        (he translated them
        himself from the English
        a year ago) outside,
        settling on the metal
        netting that protects
        the terrace from bugs,
        moths, butterflies of
        the light, fireflies, last
        night the cicada buzzing
        all night, the mockingbird
        crazily singing in the
        foliage (a cheeky
        mockingbird just like
        my country) in these
        tropics sensual nature
        dazzles among its
        creatures, it changes
        (reverses, sometimes) its
        conditions: stops reciting
        the verses of the Song of
        Enlightenment, the
        myriad insects return in
         disarray to the city (now

more remote) (the pre-dawn
hours grown darker) (they've
begun their dispersal) what
to grasp where nothing settles,
the insects have vanished
following the path of
artificial light in the distance,
the myriad depart turning
everything off (lamps,
creepy crawlies, sutras,
thoughts).

He tightens the sash at his waist. Once more straightens, lotus posture
on the canvas chair, his
grey short-sleeved shirt,
wide check pants (small
square checks) (grey cotton)
(his lower limbs could
fit twice over into this
body of fabric) fabrics
dazzle in his head, Havana,
Villegas street, multicoloured
mother of pearl buttons,
dozens of them, the cutter
runs the machine to put
in place the linings (fabrics),
fine gabardine dust, wool,
the father gazes silently
(checked cloth), the cutting
table comes back to life in
the oak wood of his native
country, thimbles,
pincushions, measuring
tape around his neck,
marking chalk made him
sneeze, silhouettes and
more silhouettes ideal

for moulding shapes, the
fields have already yielded
their harvests, the cloths take
on their form, the Dance of
the Millions is about to come
knocking on the doors, here
it freezes (in a frenzy)
syncope and bones.

For a moment he's switched on the light, closes his eyes to
avoid confusion, fixes his
gaze on the shadow
of the lamp standing
incrusted on the
terrace's (light-grey)
side wall: who is
he? where is he?
Fed up with matter,
and yet he knows
what to expect, and how
to return from night to
the living room, in
backward-looking night
how to raise his head,
stand up, find himself
once more in the
morning looking at the
Velázquez print where
the woman (yet she
seems more a man)
fries some eggs in oil
(rancid?) (clay pot) fries
in the name of all of
Spain, the boy bears
on his face the scar of
a life ruined exactly
like Spain's future, and

he, once more, sitting
down at the table, a
fruit-eater of grapes,
with his morning
glass of white
wine.

Meditation

The

attention he pays, or you could say gives, to
    the sowing of radishes,
    three rows, 14 metres long,
    is excessive. The

lack

of attention he pays to the attention he pays
    or gives to the
    rows of radishes,
    is perfect.

Meditation

With the utmost care I place a few ounces of rice in
        the clay pot. And with
        care and attention I
        boil water (circumcised)
        a pinch of salt.

Gram by gram my flesh flows reciprocally off its skeleton,
        the shape remains (I
        see it) rags of fish are
        cawing like crows
        in the branches of
        a willow tree, virgin
        pieces of a bird in a
        stampede (smooth)
        smooth in far off
        waters.

A permanent state of insatiability, there is no calm:
        what is far off (far
        off) burns, punishes,
        an immediate
        arithmetic brands me
        with its welts, wombs
        in the shape of old
        vessels, veins, stand out
        on my legs: upholding
        the heights, the sky a
        heavy etching they
        bear the weight of:
        I'm not iron, and the
        vegetation throbs
        (spreads) along my
        thighs, becomes
        stagnant puddles.

The air a heavy piece pressing down, why bother standing up,
>	you're under it.
>	I'm precise, I have outdone
>	myself: I know with
>	certainty the size of
>	what's necessary for
>	our (virulent) general needs.
>	I know it and spill out.

I have an idiot eye. My vena cava of copper or
>	plastic. Bags under my
>	eyes a shiny jet-black
>	from staring through
>	the sleep in them.

I don't dare come in from outside to the kitchen table,
>	discretion, don't say
>	a single word, there is
>	no known word: half
>	close the eyes. Moving
>	from the morsel of
>	bread I'm chewing on
>	to the glass of water to
>	the recently boiled rice.

Meditation of Kiyowara Fukayabu

Kiyowara Fukuyabu believed he was contemplating the
      (yellow) (white) new
      moon for two consecutive
      nights, remote from
      sleep, from hunger,
      he drank its rays, its
      brightness invaded his
      retinas, his inner ear, one
      by one his viscera in a
      vertical direction, the
      depths of the midget
      body which might have
      accompanied him for sixty
      years, twisted legs lit up
      by yellow, egg-yolk eyes,
      belly, knees, ankles.
      Something spills down
      the angle of the eye, a
      perpendicular pouring,
      rhomboids, polygons,
      that, breaking up, make
      waterclocks groan,
      (black) stone frogs
      leap, carp in the royal
      pond turn delirious
      with hunger, thirst, oxygen.
      Games of rings the
      motionlessness of
      Kiyowara Fukuyabu
      (few poets died so young,
      few have left a unique
      trace contained in five
      lines, thirty one
      regular syllables,

obligatory, who knows
why, from time
immemorial): the moon
for two full days the
moon unchanging
(unchanged in his stony
posture the very young
man at the death of the
already dying at his
death Fukuyabu.) To
his left, at the start of
his meditation, he saw
the bird of mists, its
wide-stretched wings
covering fir trees, willows,
the rhododendrons his
ancestors planted
at the entrance to
his stone mansion,
curved eaves, two
artesian wells, his
father's suicide
(on the Emperor's
orders), the house in
disarray, the millet
broom that stopped
casting a shadow, making
a sound. The bird flew
off, there to the left,
there, only mist
invading (disrupting) the
gaze. In the small hours
to turn one's face to the
right, to see the wagtail
alight on bushes ringed by
clover, the one spot the
(new) moon's light

doesn't touch much
less invade or
penetrate: it's about
to rain. He's about to die.
He will after all manage
to complete his twenty
five years. Some at that
moment will think of
their heartburn,
some of the need for
a chrysanthemum tea.
A fragrance of
guayacol. Camphor.
Kiyowara Fukayabu's
posture and its stone-like
nature as he slips from
his centre to the centre
of a meditation held for
forty eight hours, till he
reaches the moon's (white)
emptiness, vanishing
just as he sees himself
overtaken by the moon
beginning once more the
phases of its journey.

III

Contemplation

During the worst snowfall of the year the maple in the garden
    was covered in yellow
    panicles.

They stretched upward, I leant my back against the maple's trunk,
    I read (standing) a good
    while: golden letters
    (I was reading) gilt
    page-edges the book's
    moth-eaten spine,
    falling apart.

My head covered in white whirlybirds thighs streaked
    with (fungi)
    polyps.

My thighs in their meekness (naked) the virile
    member in woollen
    clothing (leafstalk)
    aimed at earth.

As they climb two large brown butterflies follow
    the panicles' shadow
    towards a sky-born
    tree.

And life? My mother, does she still exist? She enters with her
    bustling noise of glasses
    door-catches the
    methylene-blue tray
    thick yellow slice of
    cheese chunky bar
    of guava a pack
    already started

of biscuits
laid out
classifications
(break in).

Contemplation

The window. From the bed. Surrounded by
        virgins? Myself, or the
        third person in the
        interminable dialogue,
        with whom? A glimmer,
        of what? A way once
        and for all to interrupt
        the dialogue forever,
        in itself already
        interrupted? Inscribed
        on its wings the
        butterfly carries a few
        last words of the
        Buddha that perhaps
        no one collected. If
        I read them or my
        third person adopted
        them as a norm
        of life, it would
        change nothing.

Yesterday morning it snowed. About eleven the
        crocuses at the foot
        of the sycamore sprouted,
        the sycamore in one
        sudden flash was green,
        such instantaneous
        green I've never seen
        from the window. Cicadas
        at two in the afternoon
        till more or less five
        singing at full volume
        as the garden filled
        with dead leaves: the

sycamore stripped bare
once more, its trunk
shone in the moonlight,
bark peeled off.

Such are the mental formations of one who
without being a
contemplative
contemplates from
a large bed through
a double window
a sycamore's crown,
the change of seasons,
the new century's
(permanent) evils:
he hears galloping
(four horsemen) sees
snow fall, turns his
back to the window,
continues listening:
buds are sprouting:
cicadas singing:
sap dries: a leaf
breaks loose: spinning
round: transcribing
in an exercise book
half filled with
pictograms, Korean
letters, Japanese
swirls of symbols,
the last (unregistered)
words of the most
recent Buddha:
Mahayana: Hinayana:
the Buddha is no stranger
to manifestations.

I'm off to be a corpse. Third time this week. And it
    won't be the last. I know
    all the same how to stay
    on. In bed. Lying down.
    Buddha-style. Sideways.
    Back to the window.
    Bad omen? Not at all.
    It's where God and the
    dead leaves come in.
    A thought that I, not
    wasting any time, throw
    out. From my third
    person, as I move inwards.
    I turn on the night lamp
    on the bedside table, blue
    tulip-shaped lamp, wooden
    base, within reach. Just
    by stretching out my arm.
    This one. A slight
    trembling. Still capable,
    at my command, of
    turning on the lamp.
    Lamp is island.
    Buddha. Fearlessness
    of light. Artificial
    of course, that's alright.
    The question is seeing,
    hearing, tasting sleep's
    arrival. To touch it.
    Eyes drooping. To see
    me and see my
    third person, dressed
    in kimono, white
    socks, big eared
    (The Big-Eared One)
    my hair in a topknot
    swept up in a morion,
    my head untonsured.

And I am the Buddha in question: one more. Pure fusion
    (in a few more hours)
    of four horsemen,
    hollow gallop, four
    seasons that change
    in twenty four hours
    (I turn off the lamp)
    a big event: today
    my mental faculties
    behaved marvellously,
    what am I saying, let
    the truth be spoken,
    I've never perceived them
    so precise, so free-flowing:
    I was pleased. The
    butterfly has gone
    back to its cave (out of
    Chuang Tzu's sleep) the
    sycamore shaded the
    Buddha's final sleep,
    the crocus was the
    flower he showed his
    favourite disciple, the
    cuckoos sang in
    the oldest clocks in
    the Universe (spreading
    wide): look how
    they're sharing out two
    changes of bed
    clothes, how they're
    burning papers
    at the entrance.

IV

Satori

Hsin, of the Shingon sect, fed himself with
        his imagination during
        thirty years of a
        daily bowl
        of boiled rice.

For thirty years adding to it a few drops
        of white vinegar
        he fed himself
        licking the corners
        of his lips.

At sixty years of age and after long practice
        he chews and
        swallows (swallows)
        and chews, tasting
        nothing.

Satori

Hui-neng, tegument by tegument, penetrates the seed,
        the cells, the face in his
        mother's embryo (a girl
        of marriageable age)
        (bangles and bracelets)
        palanquin: they draw
        back the curtain of
        coarse jute, gold coins,
        expensive woods, the
        surprise on the face of
        Hui-neng's mother on the
        high wooden platform,
        thick mattress stuffed with
        a padding fragrant of tea
        roses, upholstered pillows,
        silk eiderdown, a long
        moan: some fine day or
        other the Emperor will
        recognise his bastards.

Hui-neng's gaze sadly traverses the smooth greyish
        trunk, sketch or a pure
        imagination among the
        gardens, walkways,
        amuses itself a while
        contemplating layer
        by layer the xylem,
        sapwood, concentric
        rings, the silver pendant
        earrings on the mother's
        tiny ears tinkle as
        she leans forward
        to kiss one by one
        the Emperor's fingers,

        a patchwork of
        rings: ruby, emerald,
        white gold, jade, a set
        pink pearl, yellow gold,
        in the Emperor's
        pupils: Hui-neng
        wound up glitters,
        predisposed from the
        beginning of time
        to take the leap that
        permits him to traverse
        in opposite direction
        the path from death to
        resurrection: turtle,
        armadillo, most ancient
        iguana, pupil of the (jade)
        eye, young down-and-out,
        Patriarch.

He is sitting in full lotus posture meditating at once
        the two sides of the
        leaves of the nameless
        tree that will
        illuminate his mother
        (wood womb matter)
        and the Emperor (who
        remembers in which
        annals his name is
        found?): nervation,
        parenchyma, the thick
        (inchoate) flow of sap
        can be heard held back a
        moment in the peduncle
        of the leaves (what is
        the mother assuring
        herself of? what is
        the Emperor half

corroborating?): a
sucker, as it brightens
the dogwood in one
instant will put forth
all its flowers. Ecstasy
of the Patriarch. A bad
thing. Beauty
distracts. The impetuous
flowering takes him
away from the figure
of the Buddha in the
alcove. Hui-neng
reacts to this sudden
reaction remembering
every object serves as a
base for meditation:
the little statue, the
dogwood's flower on
the verge of breaking
off or sprouting
once more; the empty
vase, half-broken
baby's toy on the shelf,
the shelf itself, its own
roughness, roughness of
a trunk or the cotyledon
that engendered his mother.

Hui-neng, at seventy, leaning on his walking stick
  from handle to tip carved
  in dogwood by
  his own hand,
  stands a long while
  emptying himself of
  the dead leaves of
  reproduction: thickets,
  lush groves, layers,

fall; membrane and
chlorophyll; from
mother the pistil, from
father the anthers.
Hui-neng rests in calm,
speculates calmly
on what calmness is
all about, steps to
take to reach it, above
all to sustain it,
and once sustained
to see it empty
itself beside the
fullness of the Void,
kidney, rectum, salivary
glands, the brain's
convolutions.

Satori

Hui-neng, sixth patriarch, raised a white cup of sake:
      dazzling light.

The porcelain cracked: sake seeped out.

He opens his mouth, closes his eyes, concludes that
      rice and its dregs
      form one and the
      same porcelain.

A single joy: the porcelain cup's dazzling light
      for one moment
      sets the spider
      trembling:
      a crack of light in
      the porcelain.

Liquid penetrates all the way down the vast inner
      sky of Hui-neng's
      entrails.

His organs, porcelain: his circulatory system,
      light: his breathing
      a liquid movement
      of spiders.

Has he reached an end? Is this absolute knowledge?

And the gift? Hui-neng is hungry (wine, there's no
      doubt, whets the
      appetite): he
      lifts to his mouth
      a handful of
      boiled rice, with

his left hand: the
right hand holds
in suspense a
white cup of sake
on the verge of
cracking.

Satori

Noin contemplates it will be for hours now some embers in the
        brazier (daisies) went
        to do something, didn't do it
        (cornflowers): did he try
        too hard? A pine tree,
        a blue tit, among
        the embers. Blue
        embers, incombustible:
        the scar in the wood
        stands out against
        Noin's fleshless
        arms, his thighs
        indistinguishable from
        wood, a mental
        lapse (augmented)
        (augmenting itself)
        the ember crumbles,
        in the whole vast
        expanse of space
        a blue tit at the ant's
        mercy, the pine
        stump at the edge of
        the ashes, Noin
        stretches out his
        hand to lift a daisy
        to his ear, his mental
        lapse increases
        (empty stitches of
        an impalpable
        wound dripping
        space).

A jump. He kicks the brazier. Scattered (coals).
        Nothing overturned.
        Neither cornflowers nor

blue tits, as if a soaring
pine tree (of rapid
growth) was going to fit
between a few embers.
Contemplation
finally drives the most
experienced crazy.
There's nothing there: no
daisies no ants lying in
wait, a few burning embers
to kill the cold a little at
the start of autumn, the
first hours of the morning.
That was (is) all. And
with joy (perhaps
excessive) Noin sees the
myriad arrive (seventy
thousand times seventy,
better than the Void): he
races around among dancing
girls, crazily strums
biwa and *samisen*, deserts first,
main course later:
water and urination
(seated) reading (cheap
literature) standing up.
Delousing, crunching
between his fingers one
by one a myriad plague
of insects. Noin cries
out that not a single
bedbug or tick is going
to be left in the whole
Universe. He pants. Lets
his hair down, what
hair? Before, there was
always something;

later, (maybe) there'll
be something. Noin
steps out, as he goes by
(zigzagging) he makes
gardens of raked pebbles
bloom, vessels of myrrh,
incense trees, and a
woman (truly, a woman)
winsome and unparalleled,
he covers her like a
hen from top to bottom
(they're the same size)
Noin gains enlightenment,
one of the princesses
of the Kingdom
shines forth.

Satori

The rollcall of the Masters goes beyond calculation:
>their concepts in no
>way complicated,
>after brief or
>prolonged meditation,
>appear trivial. That's
>all right, we have not
>been born; OK,
>knowledge must be
>accompanied by a
>a calm posture; where
>there's production
>there's destruction, no
>kidding?

As of this morning (seven on the wall clock, on and
>on, it won't stop,
>in the kitchen) I'm going
>to get rid of this fake
>monastery inside my
>body: out with the
>internal and
>external, out with
>the mountain and
>its peak. The practice
>to perform, watch
>the prices on the day's
>share market rise and
>fall on the electronic
>bar-line. And in
>the secluded park
>round the block,
>to consider (in a
>systematic way) the

housemaid showing
me her underwear from
the top of the see-saw;
a harmony of pinks
the cloudbank, the
underwear, greater
and lesser lips, little
difference between
the housemaid's vulva
and a pig.

Laziness. Total indifference. The terrace with the old easy chair.
The triclinium, watch
Rome burn. Lying back
in the easy chair on the
terrace, to contemplate
the ant's industrious
good sense. I too
to sweep away
(plan ahead) *in
mente*. My sole
business, to get out of
this existence with
what I have, to leave
home as little as
possible, abundant
indolence and little
imagination. There is
no form, to eat fruit
(in season, to favour
papaya and pineapple).
There is no sensation,
I traverse the curves of
the puffy flesh of
the housemaid in the
secluded park (arecas)
(beach grapes) (swings

and a see-saw) in my
head. In fact, the five
aggregates don't
exist, three cheers
for non-existence.
Better that than go on
burning, better than
watching your savings
disappear day by day,
answering the telephone
so some recording can
leap out trying to
sell an ointment, offer
a mortgage (moderate
interest rates) my
house has been paid off
for decades.

Satori. Or a kind of *satori*, or its cheap imitation.
Watercourses, towards
the valleys, my fly
open, shirt hanging
out, hemp shoes,
red socks. Walking.
The centre of the
Universe is Mount
Sumeru. The journey
is over. I'm only
short two kilometres,
or its equivalent in
centimetres, a point
where I can continue
the journey, if I was an
ant, in millimetres.
To reach (for a while
now I have reached):
the furthest point

of illumination.
The milk is boiling in
the saucepan: see it
doesn't evaporate. The
coffee is ready, the sugar
bowl contains two
measures of brown sugar
(I'm pleased as punch): I
catch a glimpse, (glancing
back) I catch the
conflagration, the dying
ash's break-even point still
red-hot coals.

Satori

The *arhat* knows that by smallness he reaches
        greatness: first
        error.

As long as the external voice does not dissolve
        (second error) there
        will be no
        enlightenment: for
        the *arhat* to be *arhat*.

The outer voice holds to greatness while
        the anxious spark of
        the inner voice
        persists: third error.

His eyes fixated, cursing and swearing *putana (saha)*
        (saha) they're all in it
        together: smallness
        carries implicit
        greatness just as the
        inner voice chokes up
        within the outer voice.

Years of meditation, service, *kalpas* of purifying
        the body (ablution)
        the mind (repetitions)
        day by day
        recognising the
        restlessness of
        his hands.

The *arhat's* shadow, it links up: the wall's fixed
        shadow is projected
        (a flight) on the

        departing cloud: his
        mental gaze,
        another error.

Dark spaces of greatness (waverings) in
        concentration.

Glimmers of greatness, in attrition: he sighs,
        doesn't expire, a
        scrape of air
        overloads his
        shoulders, his
        stomach relaxes.

Fire notwithstanding he rests in his humble
        meditation: ah *arhat*
        for how long.

Out of sorts, he stood up, on approaching the room's
        small window he sees
        a flower fall at the feet
        of the white ox: the
        flower fell, the ox
        indifferent to hustle
        and bustle remains calm
        in its ancestry, from the
        window a watercolour
        the (white) flower
        incrusted on the
        ox's limbs: through
        repetitions fixed
        things have
        dissolved.

Finally: the *arhat* no longer ponders, he grasps
        (a short gap) he forgets,
        timely light, timely

darkness: it has not been
in vain; in a proportion
both ascertainable and
not ascertainable the
dimensions take up
the place they take up,
the *arhat* (dissolved)
arhat (smiles): three
times he palpates
his temples left and
right, three times
(touching) forehead
and heart, he returns
to the correct posture
(that confabulation)
jewel in the lotus.

Satori

Ducks,
come
and
amuse me
in
my

blindness now I've sealed my eyes tight, like lime and stone,
        lime stings, stone hits
        very hard (to know
        what's there, obviously,
        you have to see). Deaf
        (I've walled the voices in)
        be one last barely
        palpable trace. Imagine
        I've imagined you, let's
        keep each other company,
        swap substance, I rarefied
        air, you outlines of a vapour
        trail that as they settle dissolve,
        a shimmering, an extinction:
        no darts, no arrows have
        hit, curare hasn't poisoned
        the beloved duck. I am
        in (good)

company.
I
wake.
I'm
visible.
I
can
hear

harmonies.
Ducks

enjoy my presence. Sound of an (accordion-style) canvas
        blind going up. Light jars.
        Frosty space. Microscopic
        water (not flowing)
        air where the duck glides
        to its extinction. The rhapsodist
        enters the room. The first chord,
        vibrates. And vibrates. I have
        utterly no

expectations.
Pure
animal
substance,
choral
voice

a ventriloquist's (unplugged). The rhapsodist takes charge
        of the song. Plucks the theorbo.
        The chord wavers in the air
        fearful of perpetuating
        itself; nothing to fear: it's air.
        Insubstantial. An
        incorporeal duck. Intermittent
        rhapsodist, the ornament of
        substitutions. No one is calling

down
a
curse,
admonitions
don't
exist.
One's

true
way

doesn't exist. Blindly I withdraw from my wife's womb.
       I hear warm water running,
       an echo on the fake marble
       bowl in the sink. I wash
       myself. My wife passes
       water (her legs spread)
       puts on her faded
       olive T-shirt, and I
       challenge her to dare
       to pee standing up.
       Stand up, stand up,
       try it. Loud guffaws of

laughter,
uproar
of
deluges,
universal
waters
reduced
to
refreshing

my
virile
member.

Satori

The entrance to the Temple has no entrance.

The space the *torii* would have occupied ten metres from
        the entrance is invaded
        by air that still holds
        the sounds (fragrances)
        of woodworm.

On one side of the Temple's likely access point
        the rear view of a
        gigantic statue: gold leaf
        become brass become
        soft wood become
        sounds (fragrance) of
        woodworm become air:
        a beggar with a wispy
        beard spreads half
        his body to one
        side and the other,
        his shadow no
        longer feeds
        his skinny flesh,
        he splits his own
        body backwards, the
        beggar is afraid he'll
        tumble headfirst: the
        entrance to the Temple
        has become
        inaccessible
        (unless
        non-existence
        is achieved).

First the famished mouth, then the fleshy fruit, its
        transposition into the

>
> bitter fruit of the tree
> they call neem, and next
> (the wheel speeds up,
> almost dizzying) a
> flower brushed by the
> brown veil of putrefaction:
> one by one petals break
> off in a cycle of twelve
> hours, the ants' starved
> mouth, the even more
> famished mouth of
> humus (an exhausted
> seed): the falling apart
> (for one moment) of
> Time's substance. On the
> other side of the Temple's
> likely access point, a
> gigantic tree (considered
> useable timber)
> (inexhaustible top quality
> timber) for centuries
> the statue has let slip from
> its left hand various
> microorganisms that have
> raised the tree high above
> its roots, woodworm
> doesn't yet feed itself.

In reality there was a Temple with its entrance (points
> of access) plain and hollow,
> water lying open in
> sealed stone: what wasn't
> there in reality was
> reality. Because. And
> the beggar stretching
> the palms of his hands
> upwards receives

and receives from above.
In truth. And definitively.
And nevertheless.
Because. Dark night.
The lamp has enough
of what it needs to
keep burning, on the
wall of the monastery
cell fish dance like swirls
of tar, ink smudges, the
shadows of a fern black
prancing legs: it settles
after reciting from memory
prayers from the Nirvana
Sutra, the Temple rises,
torii, the high
entrance (a gate of
heartwood) between the
undivided row of monks
(behind them) to one
side there remains a neem
tree (in flower) the
gigantic statue of
tuff that begins to
shine through.

Satori

Po Chü-I has sat down beaten and pitiful at
        the foot of the mountains,
        lost in thought: he doesn't
        look at the mountain,
        wants nothing more
        to do with the forest,
        rejects the river dumping
        its endless water,
        couldn't be bothered
        listening to the leap of
        flying fish upstream.

He is listening to a line rolling round in his head,
        discards it, with a sharp kick
        smashes the words, the
        gadfly stitches itself up,
        comes back: once again
        the moon wants to appear,
        this time in its waning
        phase, it will be necessary
        to surround it with a
        mental clarity Po Chü-I
        lost years ago (he
        feels tired) so much
        writing, a flood:
        despite long meditation
        he still hasn't reached
        enlightenment.

Or would it not be enlightenment to leave a space once
        more for the waning moon,
        allowing it to reappear on
        page seven, eleven,
        seventeen of his

     Selected Works, its
     waterlily face, its body
     a scimitar? Among
     odalisques. Apogees.
     To polish the strands of
     hair the silks of the
     ladies, the trimmed
     Joan-of-Arc-style hair,
     burnished fabric
     (clinging) to some
     flesh indifferent to
     the seated presence
     (praying mantis)
     of Po Chü-I.

Not to segregate. Not to renew or innovate. Only to execute
    a few mechanical
    movements, to become
    winding frame, waterwheel.
    Distaff. Weathervane.
    The notation the bamboo
    flute reiterates on
    the lips of a
    young woman of
    marriageable age with the
    mentality (the dress) of a
    ten year old girl. Where
    is Po Chü-I? He's
    gathering wild greens
    for the day's salad,
    at the same time to feed
    the hens: he hasn't
    read Chuang Tzu for
    five years minimum.
    And once more this
    morning he gives the
    horsefly a good slap,

    lets out a blasphemy,
    sends the moon with all its
    phases, craters, clouds and
    storms, off to
    woop woop.

Po Chü-I, what's the problem? A poem can be made
    in twenty minutes (it
    doesn't deserve any more
    time) (the horsefly)
    enters one ear, goes
    out the other (whacking
    the head out of order)
    (disorder reordered
    flows into the poem):
    the disturbance is over.
    And it's not even eight
    in the morning. You have
    the whole day ahead to
    meditate: *kensho,*
    dharani, gassho
    (learn Japanese).
    The five obstructions,
    a source of poetry (twenty
    minutes) hardly
    anything for Kuan Yin:
    between poem and the
    three hours a day of
    concentration (now
    you don't even have to
    scare off the horseflies)
    waking consists in
    contemplating (in
    successive order) pear tree,
    the pear tree's flower,
    your tunic stained
    with pear.

Satori

Elegance of Fujiwara no Teika when he
        sits for ever among
        the seamstresses
        of the Meiji era (all
        in their nineteenth
        reincarnation): the
        long dresses and
        sleeveless shirts will be
        placed on sale for the
        public to wear, doublet
        and dress lined
        with gold thread
        (indigo) (scarlet)
        (the pawlonia and the
        nameless bird) (absolutely
        no synthetic fabrics) for
        the Imperial House.

The one that in the future will lose all the wars,
        no Teika with his
        long sword, with the
        calligraphic brush,
        mantras and repetitions
        to a Buddha stubbornly
        resistant to his people,
        no Teika will not be able
        to prevent it: the exquisite
        perfectionist Fujiwara
        no Teika sets himself as
        spiritual exercise the
        manufacture of the (mass-
        produced) ideal Toyota,
        artificial silk (bargain
        price) just as good as the
        worm's loom (a savings

in the consumption of
mulberries). A military
withdrawal of bonzes, the
martial arts a game for
prepubescents and
members of the third age:
Japan has found its road
(no more need be said).

A piece of good fortune that in a few months no Teika
will reach Nirvana. His
tailbone (joy-bone)'s
more joyful than ever,
already his eyes
understand to
perfection the way of
isolating images to
discard them, his ears
hear only the prayer to
the Buddha Maitreya
(known by heart) great
glory of seeing Paradise
dissolve, moments
before (enough flashes of
light by now) the main
bedroom, the house, the key,
withdraw backwards.

Satori (Ryokan)

Every light that circumscribes a head summons
    thought.

Ryokan in shirt and tie evokes his previous reincarnation:
    tunic and halo, he could
    have dissolved yet resisted
    the temptation: and has
    reincarnated as a bureaucrat.
    A scribe. 20th Century.
    In the West (that
    indeed a tremendous
    disgrace). He doesn't
    take it to heart, whatever
    transformation *karma*
    plays on him. Ryokan
    calls to mind Mount
    Kugami, a not very
    attractive mountain apart
    from a certain bird, a fir
    tree, a tumbledown shack,
    a flower the Buddha
    showed the venerable
    Kasyapa. Ryokan doesn't
    remember a single
    word in Japanese. He
    recalls, at the end, a
    light binding his
    forehead, temples and the
    crown of his head, raising
    him slightly off the ground
    for an (opaque) half hour
    (the irreversible hour)
    piles and piles of (gusts of)
    thoughts; emptiness: all
    extinguished. That moment

he reincarnated as vermin
(an indefinite number
of times). He still knew
Japanese. Went down to
hell, lost speech. Crawled
across a space of earth of
some eight hundred (square)
metres, completely lost
the ability to show others
salvation (salvation, ugh):
Ryokan was earning points,
merit by merit he went from
slug to firefly, cuckoo, shoe
shine boy, garbage collector
(now we're in mid 20th
Century): with great
wariness, Ryokan is about
to reincarnate as an office
worker. An imperceptible
point of light recalls a
situation for him that might
direct his steps towards a
mountain, a cabin, a lake,
a single path, four books
with uncut pages, a
translation that teaches
the three arts that grant
happiness: to sit; to walk;
to stay standing. And what
does Buddha think? Statues
don't think. He lifts his
left hand to his ear like a
conch shell, maybe he
receives revelation (at least
his small slice of
information): What kind?
Is there a direct line from

Buddha to an office
worker? In one leap can a
shitty pen-pusher of papers,
blotter in hand, small-time
clerk with old-style quill,
(imaginary) tight-fitting
tunic, reach the state of
bodhisattva? He hears
scraping on paper: it must
be his father practising
calligraphy on Mount
Sumeru. It's five on the
clock: (hasty) goodbyes,
in the distance Sado, a
lamp blinking, receives
for the first time in years
an orientation; he stops;
a deer on the peak of
Kugami (frolics). He
shouts. Places himself
in profile against his own
shadow, a copy of
himself, a red shape on a
folding screen (these now
matters of the Empire).
And behind? Ryokan sticks
out his shaven head, a light
surrounds it, he is awaiting
illumination (a single gust):
one thought, not a legion.
In its place he hears
gnawing (ah if he only
had a mirror in his hand):
usually there lives on these
peaks a herbivorous
mammal, an almost
extinct species of
groundhog.

Satori

From
the
peg
hangs
saffron
the investiture
of

Buddha on the cloth, an altar, two burners for incense,
        the incense's faint perfume
        (nothing to excess)
        the room: simplicity;
        lightness; a sustained
        practice based on a
        few postures, one
        position chosen from
        five, practised for
        three weeks or an
        entire season: saffron
        in spring; a yellow that
        expires in summer; red
        giving autumn warmth;
        grey winter fabric. A few
        bowls, some wooden
        plates, two cups with no
        handles (black porcelain,
        yellow bordering) in the
        background, and behind
        that, shadows: posies,
        vine shoots (the idea
        of putrefaction)
        persistence of the weave in
        the cloths issuing from the
        imperturbable motion of

        spinning wheels. Grooves.
        Waterwheels. Looms. Flies
        come and go at a space of
        ten to twenty centimetres.
        They crash into each other.
        Take a rest. Don't stop.
        They need movement, the
        elements: and the
        whitening ecstatic
        (first) light

of
dawn.
Light
the
lucidity
of
a
fly
and the saffron investiture in the monk's tunic:
        undressed he waits for
        the moment of a still
        improbable illumination.
        Singing softly he
        probes and probes
        the series, the
        foundations, stages of a
        metamorphosis they
        captivate him. He draws
        close to distant shores, is
        about to set his feet down
        (firmly) is obliged to
        withdraw. Patience.
        He grows anxious. One
        more time, pupa, one
        more time, chrysalis: he
        waits. Tries not

             to secrete the vital
             substance that will go
             on shaping the tunic
             hanging from a peg in
             the communal room that
             for some time has
             been empty.
             For now he secretes only
             shadows: warps of a
             thread, cells of a
             honeycomb. Alveoli:
             interstices that prolong
             (patience) (patience) the
             the red-hot nature of hope,
             not how or when, only the
             leap: he gargles with
             spring water mixed half
             and half with hydrogen
             peroxide (since when
             is there hydrogen
             peroxide in a Buddhist
             monastery?): and in
             the hope, mouth
             refreshed, fly heading
             off towards the horizon
             of rubbish dumps, he

binds
his
tunic,
his
flesh
disappears
into

the saffron investiture, bundle of firewood, he lights
            the fireplace, some

embers, a fistful
of ash his respiratory
system breathes out
the final emanation

slowed down.

Satori

The marigolds that adorned the room have
        decomposed:
        splendour of
        the unfamiliar.

In the imported

ornamental Italian flowerpot whose shadow
        occupies a large part of
        the threshold, a crack:
        water begins to leak
        (shadow, of water)
        better pay attention
        or it will end up staining
        the (indelible) recently
        varnished floors.

A coin

kept with great difficulty invested itself in
        the eiderdowns (twelve
        winters ago now)
        they seem tarnished
        (unravelling) since the
        last wash.

There wasn't time for the rooster.

At dawn we found a trail of threads among
        the sheets (who would
        have thought it?).

Worse

the question of the cigars (Montecristo; a
······Churchill) that
······we brought as
······contraband
······they turned out
······worm-eaten.

The gutters

blocked up with the first autumn rains
······the old leak in the roof
······we thought repaired
······once more left a
······stain on the ceiling.

Disasters.

That bother us since we first studied the
······masters Ma Tzu,
······Lin Chi and (above all)
······(*kowtow*) Master Shen
······Hsiu: we verify the
······silence of their
······inaccessible refectories
······from our own way of
······being (deer, uncertain:
······though not indistinct)
······rag dolls under the lamp,
······probed for heartbeat:
······backlit (we meditate) in
······lotus posture
······(sand) (rock)
······(pebbles) a heavy
······shadow the body
······in the garden of
······Ryoanji.

Satori Satori Satori: since then the evenings have
 become highly
 difficult.

Satori (Ma Non Troppo)

Noin reached the highest level of
    dematerialisation
    (laughter all around
    him): he doesn't
    turn a hair. Years
    contemplating the
    wooden statue in a
    corner of the room till
    he reaches the level
    of imperturbability
    natural to the
    statue (to wood):
    it begins, *via*
    auditiva, the long
    process of the
    woodworm's activity:
    an oracle of God
    woodworm.

As a result of contemplating for years the
    wood become
    statue, What then?
    What do you mean,
    What then?
    Should he now dedicate
    light years to the
    contemplation
    of the question
    resulting from
    long contemplation
    of the wooden
    statue? Seven
    reincarnations
    for nothing?

All centred on the one
continuous, systematic,
exclusive task of
extracting the shavings
of wisdom from the
statue, from its
wood? Noin,
a vicious circle,
grabs a fistful of
(future?) sawdust
that falls from the
statue, throws
sawdust and
woodworm (should he
ask the abbot
to bless the
fistful?) to the
hens in the courtyard
(they're stupid, they eat
whatever). In its
own trajectory
thought scarcely
rouses itself, in its
course (there
on the outside)
it has begun
the destruction of
the statue, of
Noin himself,
nourishing himself on
hens (food the origin
of destruction):
procreation and
death of the
woodworm (the
wood will be over
and done with, statue

   and everything,
   caput the
   woodworm).

Those were the happiest days of Noin before his
   extinction.

Enigma of ancestors, it doesn't exist
   (the ancients'
   wisdom,
   pure nonsense).

(truly enigmas are sophistries of the mind
   if not to say
   imperial power,
   ancient wisdom
   was and will be
   mere horseshit).

Let us contemplate Noin in his last days.
   Breakfast a succulent
   (boiling hot) chicken
   soup (sweat): he's
   no fool, he doesn't
   eat sawdust
   for breakfast.
   Abdominal exercises (ten
   minutes) before
   bowel movement. He's
   sweated. Chisel, burin,
   he makes small
   wooden Buddhas,
   paints them red
   (it amuses him
   to paint one ear, for
   example, cobalt
   blue, the other

black, a black that
would frighten the
very gods of
Evil). The rest of the day,
relaxation. Reading spy
novels, when,
when will the hard
slog of death
(he's convinced it
will not be a hard slog
for him) come. Another
chicken soup.
Cuttlefish.
A medium-sized
apple. Purple
wax (how does
it happen in
a moment—which
moment?—the
most ordinary
objects change
their appearance?). To
sleep. Controlled

dream:
Buddha
reveals
spontaneous
generation
the
woodworm
scraping
slashing
above
from
inside
the

statue
(rust)
varnish
wood
base
of
copper
Noin
underneath.

Satori

He imagined, from the third person, Buddha's
    face: bat
    ears.

He went on to imagine from the second person:
    a turtle's flippers in the air
    sipping Moon and Sun,
    more sweat.

In the first person the face of Buddha appears
    as Buddha, his joy
    is limitless: the golden
    halo (from temple
    to temple binding
    his shaven head)
    makes a deafening
    sound as it sees itself
    struck (cymbals) (bat
    ears) by blind flocks:
    a flying iguana,
    a frog's coat.

He lies down, fourth person, at the foot of a stupa,
    Buddha's face, slimy
    skin, boxwood flakes:
    the ears (a part of the
    pillar of the Universe)
    reach to his knees
    (much laughter) (the
    monks split their
    sides pointing at
    him): he's lying at
    the entrance to the
    Meditation Hut, the

    morning sun flays
    him, the pre-dawn moon
    has stripped him of all
    the images he's had
    and (his joy knows
    no limit) will have.

Water clocks indicate the fifth hour, feet in the air
    the monk spins around
    dead with laughter, hides
    his head in his carapace
    (the virile member
    withdraws into his
    scrotum): he sucks in his
    belly completely (it seems
    to melt into his buttocks)
    the sun penetrates, the new
    moon penetrates, fifth
    hour and everything
    frolics (the waters
    sparkle): the sleeping
    monks shimmer where the
    flotation line melts into their
    till-then-inattentive minds.
    In a flash the young monk
    transfers his body making
    a place for it under the
    ibis, the lotus, the elephant,
    his body a turtle in its own
    right, chalk or snow-white
    lustre the face of Buddha
    (for always and ever
    pillar of the Universe).

Satori

He walked thinking of the three tons of death
        he carried on his back,
        he tripped.

The wall, the non-existent wall: he made a gesture
        (right hand) of having
        had enough, a slug
        at full speed has the
        same path (what,
        after all, will become of
        the slug, in its
        passage?)

The brambles in the ditch are raspberries (soon,
        ripening) cone-shaped
        nest in the eaves, a swift:
        a pound of honey
        comes in principle from
        a bee, you can't eat
        the bee, in the morning
        he spreads honey on a
        rice cake, joins
        his hands.

He tripped and began to lash out at the gods over
        his bruised toe-nail
        (it's half lifted) he
        leans forward and
        flies into a rage, rants
        at the stone, the
        leather of his sandals,
        each and every one of
        the gods of the
        pantheon: he's washed

>   his toe with boric
>   acid, tincture of
>   iodine, he lets himself be
>   pampered for an hour by
>   the Goddess of Mercy,
>   he changes the gauze,
>   the gauze covering his
>   eyes, will that fall? He
>   stays blind to every
>   stumble.

In the fruit bowl the raspberries darken the dining room.
>   Honey spills over the
>   rice cake. On the
>   windowsill the
>   swift plays cat and
>   mouse with the
>   Queen Mother of the
>   hive of all hives: a ton of
>   death on his back, he
>   still doesn't see
>   the earthworm's
>   inner space that
>   the swift eats nor the
>   day of the last judgement
>   for diverse creatures
>   (pushing and shoving
>   they catch his eyesight).

And will the hour arrive before he has put his house
>   in order? That too
>   doesn't matter, in
>   its own hour
>   that (frightening?)
>   event will find its order
>   by itself. By itself,
>   lotus posture, the

bruised foot on
two goose-feather
pillows, *yin* the instep,
yang the sole that's
served him for years for
wandering the
nearby mountain
paths, following
the white journey
of the ox in
the rice fields, and
soon, who cares if very
soon, he will cross in
an instant the
lake right in front
of him (has he already
walked the surface of its
waters once more?)

Satori

He adjusts his step, from dining room to bedroom.

He joins his hands, bows, that apple is enough:
    the orchard belongs
    to the community,
    the rotation of the
    seasons
    (apple orchards)
    to the gods.

He spits, blows his nose, clears his throat: eases throat
    and belly, tilts his head
    to verify the matter
    surrounding him is
    reduced to its
    minimal expression:
    mug, basin,
    bowl, paper,
    inkwell, three
    thick volumes
    (read in rotation
    as words
    dissolve words): a print
    hangs from the
    side wall (four
    fixed walls).
    He relaxes. Adjusts
    his gaze, to the front.
    Avoids. If they ask him
    he would have to
    concentrate to reply
    if his robe is
    saffron, if he's
    totally naked,

or if he's wearing
the shiny cloth that
covers his privates.
He's finished eating
the apple. Gong.
Later he will step out
to bury its seeds
(part of a certain
ritual) of course
it won't give birth
to an apple: the gods
have already given
everything, there's
nothing to ask for.

There are three questions: what time is it? where is he?
how to enter
the Mansion of
the Immortals? The third
question depends on the
second. The second
question has no answer
(the answer would not
correspond to the real
solution the third question
seeks). I am here it
doesn't make the
Mansion or its entrance
door appear. I am
here, in a room made
of rice paper and hemp,
the clear substance
of the entrance door to
the Mansion does
not appear: it's
eight in the morning
exactly. Do you want

anything more unreal?
Can an eternal door be
made of hemp or rice
paper? Eight in the
morning.

(Kneeling) he rests his arms on the windowsill:
a map visible. Pupil,
apple-seed, the apple from
the orchard, orchards
and gods, Taishan, a
yellow river and a river
of red water: world's
end (they pulsate)
(celestial music?)
(will the spheres open?)
his knees hurt
(the scrape still
burns) (will the
floodgates open?). Was
it necessary, as on every
morning, to pose the
three questions? Three
books are resting on the
pinewood footstool. The
recently washed brass
bowl shines in the washing
up basin. The basin
reveals a black stain (he's
never spilt it, the ink).
Why ask? He goes out, at
a pace, a regular pace,
towards the small city's
municipal park, the three
temples, the avenue
of trees all pruned
to the same height: on his

return, eleven in the
morning, he fills the rice
sack, the jar of honey,
the two ink-pots
(Prussian blue and its
shadow) replaces
the ream of paper, refills
the receptacle of rice wine.
On the footstool, nine
thick volumes (always
the same mistake) he
sits down. Joins his
hands. Sings softly to
himself, his head
thinning on one side, he
waits for the cessation of
his voice to start again
(hunger) (writing)
(ablution) the
unshakeable (daily) task
of inclinations.

Satori

Overnight

my pubic hair

white.

Satori

Under the hundred year old rubber tree the patriarch
        receives revelation.

The patriarch will be one hundred years old the tree
        a thousand.

The patriarch scratches his head the breeze that
        rocks the leaves of the
        rubber tree propels
        smooth skiffs
        ocean surfaces
        the glittering of a
        wake: now the patriarch
        (things of revelation)
        has boarded (in the
        opening and closing of
        an eye) the Boat.

In the background, where the Earth is flat, he has
        already fallen off the edge.

And with him, the (thousand year old) rubber tree:
        things that are a part
        of all revelation. And
        of what's revealed that
        in its legible part says
        (says to the patriarch):
        it was a spider's thread
        a mere suppuration that
        had for a moment
        seemed to separate beings
        and things, the thread
        alone was indistinct.

With the patriarch under the rubber tree at the point of
        (setting sail) receiving
        enlightenment
        there fell off the edge
        in strict alphabetical
        order Buddha
        dazzling light
        patriarch revelation
        and rubber tree.

Satori

The

monk put on some socks with more colours than
      the rainbow, a
      pink kimono with
      ideograms in three
      colours, from the most
      lurid black to a vanishing
      white: *obi*
      bottle-green. And
      stained denim pants,
      hems unravelling,
      stitched-up holes on
      the thighs, brown
      patch on the right
      knee, a real joy
      to behold. Is the monk no
      longer a monk? Will he
      receive a reprimand from
      from the abbot? Will
      devas and birds laugh as
      he goes by? He walks once
      round the cast-iron statue
      of Buddha seated, ruby
      on the forehead, legs of
      verdigris, red eyes, the
      topknot chocolate-coloured.
      Is Buddha no longer
      Buddha? Should he fear a
      strong reprimand from
      some middling abbot,
      maybe the most violent
      reprimand? The monk
      hooks a long ear-ring

to his left ear, pretends
to place the other (a
trembling chandelier)
in Buddha's right
ear lobe. As a dare,
normality will be
spread among all the
creatures of the globe:
we won't be able to
distinguish gems from
fake jewellery, the cicada
from the itinerant
rhapsodist singing from
town to town (in
monochord) thousand
year old *sutras* now
almost without meaning.
Praying to Buddha is as
good as peeling an orange.
The monk, who knows if
from contrition,
indifference or wisdom,
puts on the grey socks of
meditation: puts on the
saffron robe, adjusts its
fabric to his skin, and
after the prescribed
circumambulation of
the (imperishable) stone
statue sits opposite
Buddha, stops all
inner imaginations,
sinks into the stone that
becomes more and more
porous, reaches the
point of concentration
where there exists on the

    very edge of dissolving
    a single colour, substance
    and of the fiction of
    substance only a vague

conception.

V

Satori

The worm
(unrepentant)
(one more aspect of
the interrogation of
God) is considered
without hesitation
(efficient) cause
of the apple's
destruction.
Not true.
Not true.
It drills its way
(moves forward)
in full knowledge that
the apple
offers it
a full-fleshed
body
(of redemption).

Satori

I'm
going
to
be
born
in
mama's
placenta

    a zen monk head shaved sweeping with millet
        broom the entrance to
        the third monastery in
        a row far away at the
        back: beyond it nothing, all
        vanished

the
curving
mountains
the
roads
the
circling

    turns of the vulture waiting for my birth so
        that I may finish
        sweeping mother
        has become
        contemplative she
        is crouching to listen to
        the persistent noise
        on the even ground
        at the entrance of
        the third monastery

in a row at the exit
by the western gate
of Kyoto: over
time

the
precepts
have
shrunk
to
a
maximum
of

three: to sweep as an exercise in creating stability;
        with your own eyes,
        to forge the vulture's
        slow circles in the air
        (maximum height) so that,
        with the community of
        monks, you may
        exemplify the relativity of
        facts; to pile up the
        sweepings and leave
        them to rot (leaves dust
        ground-up pebbles
        fruiting juniper cones
        a smashed bowl
        porcelain chips
        bronze rust) a
        token of fragility:
        fragile substance's
        enduring relativity
        in the steady rhythm
        achieved by mama's

separated
thighs
in
her
struggle
(releasing
me)
in

    the placenta so I might be born for the last
           time a Zen monk on the
           outskirts of Kyoto
           2006 common era
           her participation now
           over, mine soon to
           finish. Flesh
           embers. Bone
           embers. Viscera
           after viscera of
           exhaustion. The rule
           ordains that the
           broom rest against
           the monastery façade
           on the right-hand side
           (to freshen up). On
           entering, a light bow
           of the head, join your
           hands quickly in such a
           way that you don't
           notice it yourself. Breakfast.
           Natural functions.
           Participation. Withdrawal.
           To lean, with or without a
           shadow of one's own, due
           to one's age. And here
           the voice that reduces

all to dust, brings me back
to reality, inviting me to

help
set
the
table
fold
the
clothing
kindly drop all this nonsense.

Portrait of a Seventy-year-old and an Adolescent

Ikkyu, seventy years old (and a good deal more) myopic,
>	lets the creases of his face
>	(and other folds of skin)
>	be felt by Mori, fourteen
>	years old, blind from
>	birth: Mori (Jap.,forest)
>	lets the sparse wisps of
>	her pubescent fuzz be
>	touched by the stiffened
>	fingers of Ikkyu, Ikkyu is
>	gathering blueberries,
>	scavenges from the
>	depths two juicy
>	blackberries, (ostrich-like)
>	sinks his tongue (a
>	passageway) among
>	the first buds of
>	bamboo: the ibis
>	gazing at them flaps
>	its wings, and distracts
>	them for a moment.

Mori places on the grass the coarse serge tablecloth,
>	Ikkyu recounts the
>	movements of a dragonfly
>	skimming the water: Mori
>	is frightened (she fears
>	the dragonfly will drown)
>	Ikkyu calms her with
>	a kiss on each
>	temple. Thick
>	and bile-scented. After
>	the second glass of wine

he will describe the
gallantries (last night)
under a star-studded sky
of fireflies on heat
intermittently fornicating
among a field of
clover. The birth of
bees. Resuscitation
of flies. The fixed
way a flower has
of once more
being a flower.

Mori, only feeling with her hands, with unimaginable
precision places two
ceramic cups (with no
handles) the carafe of
wine, two deep wooden
bowls; and from a
basket of unfathomable
concavity, corn
bread, thick strips
of yellowtail *au
naturel*, sauces with
wasabi and soy base, from
now on Ikkyu must restrict
his consumption of salt:
paté. Truffles. A bowl of
rice and black beans. The
crafted perfection of two
crustaceans. The bottle of
rum (aged five years). Two
ice-cold Sapporo.
Crema catalana.
Small guayaba cakes.
Sweet potato dessert.
Two cigars (thick-sized;

short) blue mountain
coffee.

The power of a stallion inside Mori, *satori:* ten
minutes. Zen, ravines
and watercourses of
deboned flesh inside
Mori. Are digested.
Separated; excreted.
A swarm of voracious
locusts banquets
three times a day on
their bodies: knobbly
walking stick, Ikkyu;
tight-fitting tulle,
Mori. Night falls (for
Ikkyu only, obviously)
they sit on
a floor of worn
rush mats, one
naked back against the
other, full-fleshed against
coarse and wrinkled,
this one budding forth
against that one, already
fixed, slipping away: Mori
notices the natural work
of progression,
Ikkyu growing bolder,
all-controlling pendulum
of the Universe,
enters her.

www.ingramcontent.com/pod-product-compliance
Lightning Source LLC
Chambersburg PA
CBHW031153160426
43193CB00008B/345